US MILITARY

NIGHT STALKERS

BY CHARLES MARLIN

WWW.APEXEDITIONS.COM

Apex is distributed by North Star Editions:
sales@northstareditions.com | 888-417-0195

Produced for Apex by Red Line Editorial.

Photographs ©: Luke Sharrett/Getty Images News/Getty Images, cover; Mass Communication Specialist 1st Class Daniel Gaither/US Navy/DVIDS, 1, 26–27; Staff Sgt. Brandon J. White/US Army/DVIDS, 4–5, 6–7; Tech. Sgt. Carly Feliciano/US Air Force/DVIDS, 8–9; Senior Airman Ty Pilgrim/US Air Force/DVIDS, 10–11; Maj. Jeff Slinker/DVIDS, 12–13; Cpl. Kyle McNally/US Marine Corps/DVIDS, 14–15; Staff Sgt. Nikki Felton/US Army/DVIDS, 16–17; Staff Sgt. Gaelen Lowers/US Army/DVIDS, 19, 29; Lance Cpl. Seth Rosenberg/US Marine Corps/DVIDS, 20–21; Senior Airman Johnny Diaz/US Air Force/DVIDS, 22–23; Airman 1st Class Hussein Enaya/US Air Force/DVIDS, 24; Pfc. Joshua Fish/US Army/DVIDS, 25

Library of Congress Control Number: 2025939216

ISBN
979-8-89250-806-3 (hardcover)
979-8-89250-835-3 (paperback)
979-8-89250-890-2 (ebook pdf)
979-8-89250-864-3 (hosted ebook)

Printed in the United States of America
Mankato, MN
012026

NOTE TO PARENTS AND EDUCATORS

Apex books are designed to build literacy skills in striving readers. Exciting, high-interest content attracts and holds readers' attention. The text is carefully leveled to allow students to achieve success quickly. Additional features, such as bolded glossary words for difficult terms, help build comprehension.

TABLE OF CONTENTS

CHAPTER 1

SNATCH 'N' GRAB

A car drives down an empty road. Suddenly, a shadow passes overhead. A helicopter zooms past. It's an MH-6 Little Bird. It lands and blocks the road.

An MH-6 Little Bird helicopter can fly 175 miles per hour (282 km/h).

Another Little Bird lands behind the car. Soldiers rush out of both helicopters. The soldiers are Night Stalkers. They run toward the car with guns drawn.

SMALL AND SILENT

Little Birds are small and light. They don't make much noise. And they can land in tight spaces. They may drop troops onto rooftops or bridges.

Soldiers often sit on benches attached to a Little Bird's side doors. These soldiers can quickly leave the aircraft.

The Night Stalkers pull an enemy leader out of the car. They bring him into one of the helicopters. Then they take off again.

A Little Bird can fly up to 288 miles (463 km) without stopping.

FAST FACT

Surprise attacks to catch enemies are called "snatch 'n' grab" missions.

CHAPTER 2

HISTORY

Night Stalkers are part of the US Army. The team was founded in 1981. It often works with other **special ops** soldiers. It helps them move and attack.

"Night Stalkers" is a nickname. The group's full name is the 160th Special Operations Aviation Regiment.

For example, the Night Stalkers fought in the Persian Gulf War (1990–1991). They brought soldiers into enemy areas. They also destroyed enemy weapons.

DARK DROPS

Night Stalkers often fly in darkness. They may sneak soldiers or supplies into war zones. Or they may rescue people who are trapped or captured. They also spy on enemies.

Night Stalkers often jump out of helicopters. During some missions, they land in water.

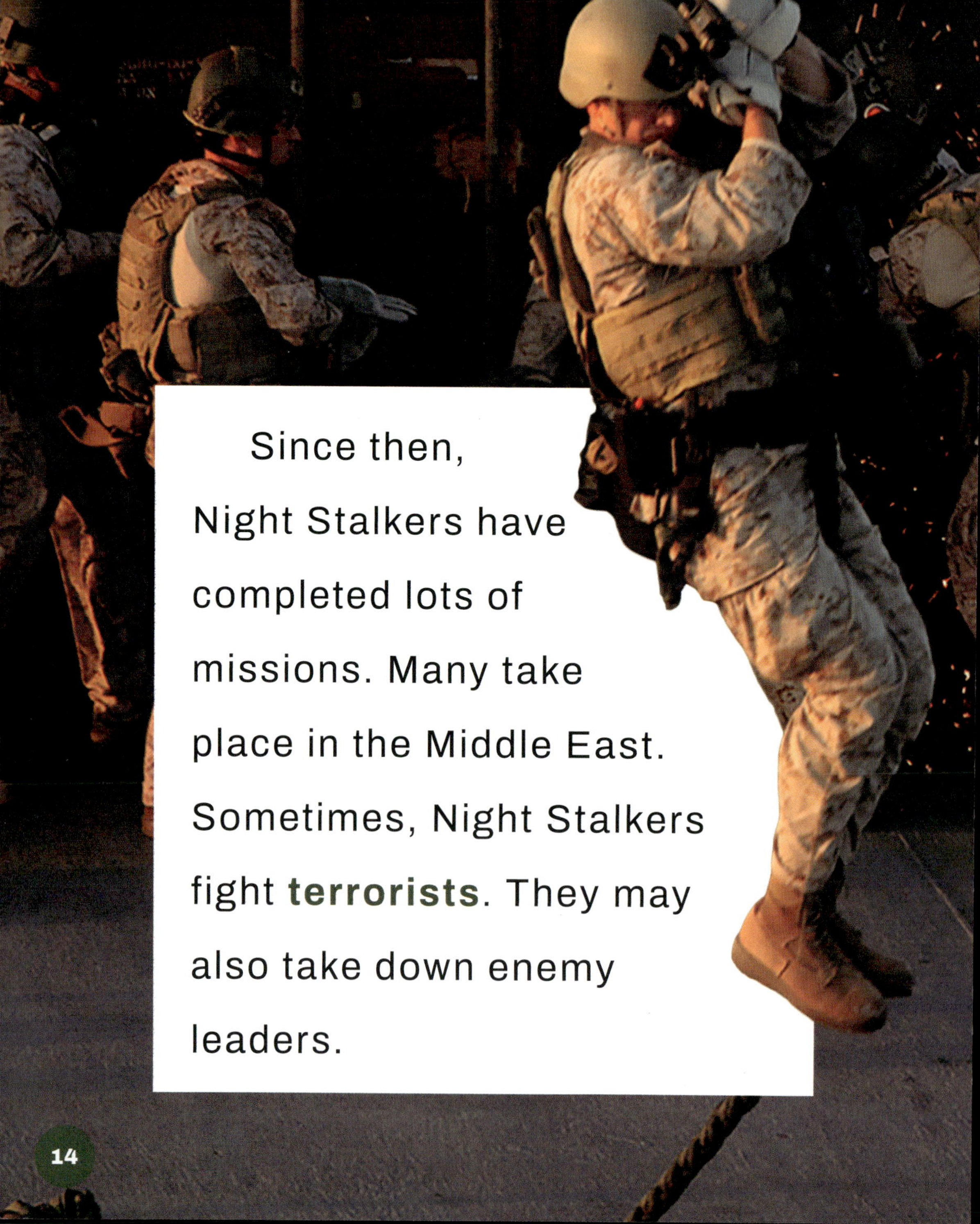

Since then, Night Stalkers have completed lots of missions. Many take place in the Middle East. Sometimes, Night Stalkers fight **terrorists**. They may also take down enemy leaders.

FAST FACT

The team's **motto** is "Night Stalkers don't quit."

During some missions, Night Stalkers help soldiers board ships to search for illegal items.

CHAPTER 3

TOUGH TRAINING

Soldiers apply to join the Night Stalkers. Only the top candidates get picked. Soldiers must be fit and strong. They need **security clearance**, too.

Night Stalkers must be between 17 and 35 years old.

Chosen soldiers go through a training course. They swim and run long distances. They practice shooting and **navigating**. Tests also check how they think and act under stress.

FAST FACT

Up to 60 percent of soldiers may fail to complete the training course.

The training course lasts a few weeks. It is called "Green Platoon."

After basic training, soldiers learn **specialized** skills. They carry out practice missions. And they train to face many kinds of danger.

Soldiers may practice refueling aircraft at night.

TYPES OF TASKS

Some Night Stalkers are pilots. Others become crew members. They focus on weapons or medical care. Still others have support roles. They help with **communication** and planning.

CHAPTER 4

MISSION TIME

The Night Stalkers are based in Fort Campbell, Kentucky. But they carry out missions around the world. The team is split into four groups called battalions.

During Operation Polar Dagger, Night Stalkers picked up Navy SEALs from Alaska.

Each battalion includes a few hundred soldiers. Teams fly high-tech helicopters. The Black Hawk is one example. It has large guns and powerful **sensors**.

The MH-60M Black Hawk can fire several types of large guns.

FAST FACT

Night Stalkers sometimes operate Gray Eagles. These drones can help with spying or attacks.

Drones such as Gray Eagles don't carry pilots. Instead, people steer them from a distance.

Night Stalkers often fly in bad weather. They have to hide from enemies, too. Sometimes they fly low to the ground. This helps them stay off **radar**.

FAST-ROPING

Night Stalkers often use fast-roping to drop troops. Thick ropes hang down from helicopters. Soldiers slide down them to reach the ground.

Fast-roping lets Night Stalkers drop soldiers in enemy areas without landing their helicopters.

COMPREHENSION QUESTIONS

Write your answers on a separate piece of paper.

1. Write a few sentences explaining the types of missions Night Stalkers do.
2. If you were a Night Stalker, would you want to be a pilot, crew member, or support person? Why?
3. When did the Night Stalkers form?
   - A. 1981
   - B. 1991
   - C. 1993
4. Why would Night Stalkers want to stay off radar?
   - A. Radar could stop helicopters from flying.
   - B. Radar could warn enemies about an attack.
   - C. Radar only works during the day.

5. What does **candidates** mean in this book?

*Soldiers apply to join the Night Stalkers. Only the top **candidates** get picked.*

- **A.** people who quit something
- **B.** people who try to get a job
- **C.** people who are not skilled

6. What does **roles** mean in this book?

*Still others have support **roles**. They help with communication and planning.*

- **A.** types of helicopters
- **B.** types of jobs
- **C.** types of food

Answer key on page 32.

GLOSSARY

communication

Sending and receiving messages.

motto

A short sentence or phrase that describes a group's beliefs.

navigating

Finding one's location and planning which way to go.

radar

A system that sends out radio waves to locate objects.

security clearance

Official permission to see or hear information that the government keeps secret from most people.

sensors

Tools that take in information, such as sounds or movement.

specialized

Involving extra focus, skill, or training.

special ops

Military groups or missions requiring extra skills and training.

terrorists

People who attack and scare others to reach their goals.

TO LEARN MORE

BOOKS

Banks, Anita. *US Army*. Apex Editions, 2023.

Hamilton, John. *United States Army*. Abdo Publishing, 2021.

Marlin, Charles. *Helicopters*. Apex Editions, 2025.

ONLINE RESOURCES

Visit **www.apexeditions.com** to find links and resources related to this title.

ABOUT THE AUTHOR

Charles Marlin is an author, editor, and avid cyclist. He lives in rural Iowa.

INDEX

ANSWER KEY:
1. Answers will vary; 2. Answers will vary; 3. A; 4. B; 5. B; 6. B